THE EGG-CELLENT EASTER Activity BOOK

Buster Books

ILLUSTRATED BY KATHRYN SELBERT
WRITTEN AND EDITED BY LARA MURPHY
DESIGNED BY ZOE BRADLEY
COVER DESIGNED BY ANGIE ALLISON

First published in Great Britain in 2022 by Buster Books, an imprint of
Michael O'Mara Books Limited, 9 Lion Yard, Tremadoc Road, London SW4 7NQ

W www.mombooks.com/buster   f Buster Books   🐦 @BusterBooks   📷 @buster_books

ISBN: 978-1-78055-817-2

1 3 5 7 9 10 8 6 4 2

This book was printed in January 2022 by Bell & Bain Limited,
303 Burnfield Road, Thurnliebank, Glasgow,
G46 7UQ, United Kingdom

FSC
www.fsc.org

MIX
Paper from
responsible sources
FSC® C007785

AN EASTER EGGS-TRAVAGANZA!

Get your puzzling hat on and have a crack at this exciting collection of Easter-themed games and activities. Packed with cheeky chicks, bouncing bunnies and lolloping little lambs, this book is bursting with hours of Easter fun.

There are egg-hunt mazes, cute colouring challenges, spot the differences, search-and-find scenes, logic games and many more. All the answers are at the back of the book, if you get stuck.

Good luck and hoppy puzzling!

SPRING CHICKENS

These cute chicks are enjoying the spring sunshine.
Can you spot eight differences between the two pictures?

BEAUTIFUL BONNET

Which shadow matches this pretty
Easter bonnet exactly?

A.

B.

C.

D.

E.

5

FLOWER POWER

Can you match up the pairs of flowers that look the same? Which flower is not one of a pair?

CRACKED!

Can you work out which five pieces below fit together to make the complete Easter egg?

RABBIT WARREN

Which bunny is on the path that leads to the big Easter egg?
Help the rabbits through the underground maze to find out.

A.

B.

C.

D.

9

EASTER COOKIES

Decorate and colour in these yummy
Easter cookies any way you like!

10

LOST LAMB

Help this sheep munch his way through the meadow
by following the flowers in the order below.
You can move across, up and down, but not diagonally.

ORDER TO FOLLOW:

COUNTING CHICKS

How many little chicks can you
count in this picture?

ODD EGG OUT

All of these Easter eggs look the same,
apart from one — can you spot it?

EGG HUNT

These mice are having an Easter egg hunt! Count how many
of each egg in the checklist you can spot hidden in the scene.
Do your totals match the ones shown?

CHECKLIST:

14

COUNT THE CARROTS

How many carrots can you count in this jumble?

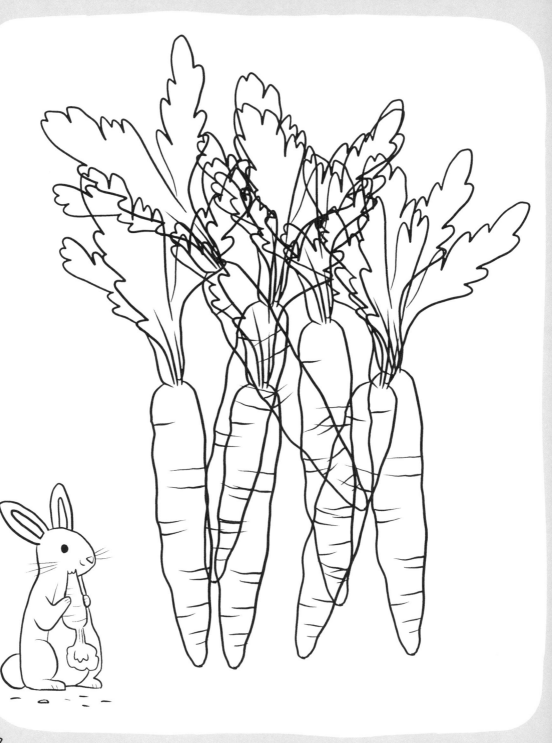

EASTER BOUQUET

Which group below contains everything you need to make the pretty Easter basket on the left?

A.

B.

C.

D.

POND PUZZLER

Which two tiles below do not match this pond scene?
Can you spot three eggs hidden in the main picture, too?

A.

B.

C.

D.

E.

LITTLE LAMBS

Some of these lambs are small and some are much bigger.
Can you put them in order of size, from smallest to largest?
Write the correct order in the spaces below.

....

....

COLOUR ME!

Colour in this egg-tastic
Easter wreath.

MEADOW MEMORY

Study this picture of a pretty spring meadow for two minutes. Then turn the page and see how much you can remember about it.

MEADOW MEMORY (CONTINUED)

Once you've looked at the picture on the previous page, see if you can answer these questions without turning back.

1. How many butterflies are there in the picture?

....

2. How many caterpillars are there in the picture?

....

3. What is one of the caterpillars eating?

....

4. True or false? All of the bees are sitting on flowers.

....

5. Is the ladybird at the top of the picture or at the bottom?

....

6. True or false? One of the Easter eggs has a spotty pattern on it.

....

WHOSE EGG IS WHOSE?

Can you follow the footprints to work out
which egg belongs to which chicken?

BUSY BUNNIES

Each bunny has a pattern on it that matches a pattern in one of the baskets. Look closely at the pictures to match each bunny with the correct basket.

CLOSE-UP SHOP

There are lots of Easter goodies on display in this shop window. Can you find and circle each of the close-ups at the bottom of the page in the main picture?

A.

B.

C.

D.

E.

F.

25

TREE TEASER

Can you spot ten differences between
the two pictures of this Easter tree?

HATCHING CHICKS

Three baby birds have hatched from their shells! Join
the dots from 1 to 50 to complete the picture.

MOUSY MIX-UP

These little mice have lost their Easter bonnets. Can you work out which bonnet belongs to which mouse? Write the correct name under each bonnet.

SQUEAK
"My bonnet has more than two eggs and no carrots."

MAGNUS
"My bonnet has carrots but no eggs."

OZZY
"My bonnet has eggs and isn't Squeak's."

JERRY
"My bonnet has feathers but no birds."

NIBBLES
"My bonnet has the most flowers."

EGG TRAIL

It's Easter morning and the Easter Bunny is busy hiding chocolate eggs. Follow the coordinates to find the golden egg — then colour it in!

1. Start at A1
2. Move 3 squares UP to A4
3. Move 3 squares RIGHT to D4
4. Move 3 squares UP to D7
5. Move 2 squares RIGHT to F7
6. Move 2 squares DOWN to find the golden Easter egg

7.
6.
5.
4.
3.
2.
1.

A.   B.   C.   D.   E.   F.   G.

30

Which square is the golden Easter egg hidden in? ....

PERFECT PATTERNS

Look closely at the springtime sequences below.
Can you fill in the missing items to complete the patterns?

WHICH EASTER ANIMAL ARE YOU?

If you were an animal, what would you be?
Answer the questions to find out!

START

You're building a new home. Where would it be?

Anywhere with a great view.

What kind of friend are you?

I have just a few close friends.

Where do you want to go on holiday?

I like to talk to lots of different people.

It's your birthday. What would you like to do?

Deep in the woods.

You're planning a day trip with friends. Where do you go?

Somewhere we can swim.

Anywhere with secret places to explore.

Which superpower would you choose?

Anywhere with
a pool.

→ Duck

Somewhere wild
with lots of trees.

→ Sparrow

If I can sunbathe,
I'm happy.

→ Hen

Have a party with lots
of food and fun!

→ Squirrel

Go on an adventure
somewhere new.

→ Dragonfly

To breathe
underwater.

→ Frog

Invisibility.

→ Mouse

To be super-quick
on my feet.

→ Rabbit

BEAUTIFUL BUNTING

These Easter decorations are looking rather bare!
Add the finishing touches by colouring them in.

HOMEWARD BOUND

Guide this bumblebee back home through the flowers.
Can you make the journey, while only landing on numbers
next to each other in the two-times table?

Finish

MORNING MAYHEM

These pairs of egg cups are ready for Easter breakfast, but one is missing its matching partner. Can you spot it?

PUZZLING PICNIC

Look carefully at this picnic hamper packed with Easter goodies. Try to remember as much of the scene as possible, then turn the page and test your memory!

PUZZLING PICNIC
(CONTINUED)

Once you've looked at the picture on the previous page, see if you can answer these questions without turning back.

1. What type of large fruit was in the picture?

....

2. How many Easter eggs did you count?

....

3. True or false? Three cupcakes were missing icing.

....

4. Which type of cutlery was missing from the scene — knives, forks or spoons?

....

5. True or false? There were two bees at the top of the picture.

....

6. The square sandwiches have been cut in half to make what shape?

....

MIRROR IMAGE

These animals are keeping cool by the pond — but their reflections are missing. Draw in the missing reflections to complete the picture. One has been done for you.

BLOOMING BLOSSOM

There are fifteen birds hiding around this spring blossom tree. Can you spot them all?

40

EQUAL EGGS

Each basket contains five Easter eggs, but some of the patterns are missing. Can you draw in the missing designs so each basket contains an egg of every pattern?

HOP TO IT!

Can you help the frog hop across the pond to the giant Easter egg? You can only step on the lily pads that have six sides and are next to each other.

Start

Finish

43

SNAIL TRAIL

These snails have been eating their fill of delicious plants. Can you follow the trails to work out what each snail ate, and which snail missed out on lunch?

A.

B.

C.

D.

E.

F.

1.

2.

3.

4.

5.

6.

CRAFT-ASTROPHE!

Easter crafting can be a messy business! Can you spot the eight differences between the two scenes below?

TOPPLING TOWERS

Can you fill in the missing numbers in each sequence on these Easter egg towers? Start at the bottom and work your way up.

Tower 1 (left, bottom to top): 6, 9, 12, ___, 18, 21, ___

Tower 2 (middle, bottom to top): 10, 20, 30, 40, ___, ___, 70

Tower 3 (right, bottom to top): ___, 11, 13, 15, ___, 19, 21

PUDDING PUZZLER

Easter baking has caused chaos in the kitchen. Can you work out
which of the four jigsaw pieces is missing from the picture below?

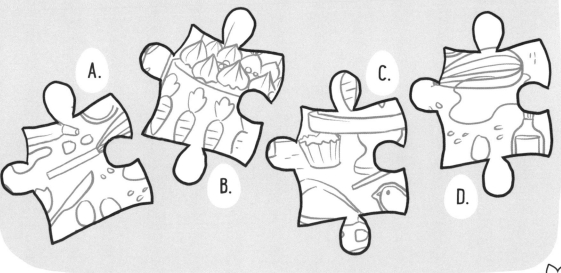

A.

B.

C.

D.

COLOUR CRAZY

These Easter cards have been left unfinished.
Decorate and colour them in to finish them off.

CHEEKY CHICK

Help this little chick through the maze to the finish line.
How many eggs do you pick up on your way? If you
bump into a mother hen, go back to the start!

Start

Finish

DASHING DUCKS

It's getting busy down by the river. How many ducks can you count in this scene?

GAME ON!

Race to the finish line, collecting Easter eggs along the way. You'll need a dice and a counter for each player. Take turns to roll the dice and move your counter along the path. Watch out for the smashed eggs!

The Easter Bunny is running late. **Move back one space.**

It's a sunny Easter day. **Move forward two spaces.**

You give an Easter gift to a friend. **Move forward to the finish line.**

Finish

Start

You find two Easter eggs. Move forward two spaces.

Your spring flowers are blooming. Move foward one space.

You drop two eggs. Move back two spaces.

You spot the Easter Bunny! Move forward three spaces.

You drop your Easter basket. Move back three spaces.

WHO'S THE REAL EASTER BUNNY?

Only one of these bunnies is the real Easter Bunny.
Can you work out which one it is from the clues below?

1. The Easter Bunny has an even number of eggs.
2. The Easter Bunny has its eyes open.
3. The Easter Bunny isn't nibbling something.

ANSWERS

PAGE 4: SPRING CHICKENS

PAGE 5: BEAUTIFUL BONNET

Answer: C

PAGE 6: FLOWER POWER

PAGE 7: CRACKED!

PAGE 11: LOST LAMB

PAGES 8–9: RABBIT WARREN

Answer: B

PAGE 12: COUNTING CHICKS

Answer: 17

PAGE 13: ODD EGG OUT

PAGE 16: COUNT THE CARROTS
Answer: 7

PAGE 17: EASTER BOUQUET
Answer: C

PAGE 18: POND PUZZLER
Answer: C and D

PAGES 14–15: EGG HUNT

PAGE 19: LITTLE LAMBS

B, G, A, E, C, D, F

PAGES 21–22: MEADOW MEMORY

1. There are 5 butterflies in the picture.

2. There are 3 caterpillars in the picture.

3. One of the caterpillars is eating the petal of a flower.

4. False, most of the bees are flying.

5. The ladybird is at the top of the picture.

6. False, neither of the Easter eggs has a spotty pattern.

PAGE 23: WHOSE EGG IS WHOSE?

Chicken A – 1
Chicken B – 4
Chicken C – 2
Chicken D – 3

PAGE 24: BUSY BUNNIES

Basket A – Bunny 2
Basket B – Bunny 1
Basket C – Bunny 3
Basket D – Bunny 4

PAGE 25: CLOSE-UP SHOP

PAGES 26–27: TREE TEASER

PAGE 28: HATCHING CHICKS

PAGE 29: MOUSY MIX-UP

1. Squeak
2. Ozzy
3. Nibbles
4. Magnus
5. Jerry

PAGE 31: PERFECT PATTERNS

PAGE 30: EGG TRAIL

Answer: F5

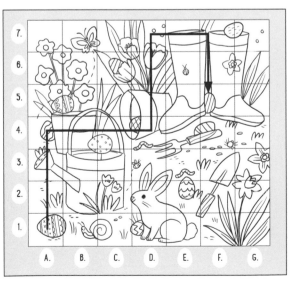

PAGE 35: HOMEWARD BOUND

PAGES 36: MORNING MAYHEM

PAGE 39: MIRROR IMAGE

PAGES 37-38: PUZZLING PICNIC

Answers:
1. A pineapple.
2. Six Easter eggs.
3. False, two cupcakes are missing icing.
4. The knives are missing.
5. False, there is one bee.
6. The sandwiches are cut into triangles.

PAGE 40: BLOOMING BLOSSOM

PAGE 41: EQUAL EGGS

Each basket should contain 1 spotty egg,
1 flowery egg, 1 squiggly egg, 1 striped egg
and 1 mixed-pattern egg.

PAGES 42-43: HOP TO IT!

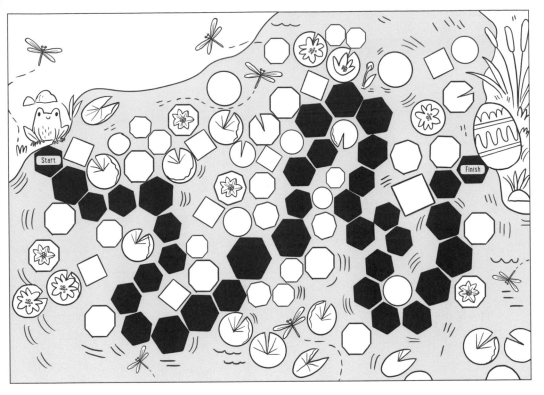

PAGE 44: SNAIL TRAIL

A ate plant 4, B ate plant 3, D ate plant 2, E ate plant 6, F ate plant 5 and C missed out on lunch.

PAGE 45: CRAFT-ASTROPHE!

PAGE 46: TOPPLING TOWERS

6, 9, 12, 15, 18, 21, 24
10, 20, 30, 40, 50, 60, 70
9, 11, 13, 15, 17, 19, 21

PAGE 47: PUDDING PUZZLER

C.

PAGE 50: CHEEKY CHICK
You pick up six eggs along the way.

PAGE 51: DASHING DUCKS
Answer: 14

PAGES 54-55: WHO'S THE REAL EASTER BUNNY?